WHEN DIGITAL ISN'T REAL

Fact Finding Offline for Serious Writers

Marlene Samuels, PhD

Published in 2013 by CreateSpace Independent Publishing Platform

ISBN-10: 149107146X
ISBN-13: 978-1491071465

Dedication:

My greatest thanks go to University of Chicago where I learned more about the research process than most people (myself included), would ever believe exists. The wonderful and unanticipated benefit of my many years spent at the University, slugging away towards my PhD was an opportunity to experience, first hand, dramatic transformations in research from card catalogues to online searches and to be able to recognize both the benefits and drawbacks of each.

Marlene B. Samuels
Chicago, Illinois
August 2013

Crescat scientia; vita excolatur
Let knowledge grow from more to more;
and so be human life enriched.

Doing research on the Web is like using a library assembled piecemeal by pack rats and vandalized nightly.

-Roger Ebert

Contents

Let's consider Gilbert and Sullivan's wise words regarding the importance of details in the stories we tell.

It's all about adding an air of verisimilitude to an otherwise bald and unconvincing narrative.

The Mikado or The Town of Titipu. (An opera in two acts.)
Arthur Sullivan and W. S. Gilbert. 1885. London, England.
Interpretation by Lawrence R. Samuels.

Preface

Fifteen years ago Penguin-Berkley Books offered to publish my mother's World War II memoir, *The Seamstress: A Memoir of Survival.* I was ecstatic. After all, at that point the manuscript had spent more than eighteen years in my desk drawer. It had been there since my mother's death eighteen years earlier.

The editor at Penguin-Berkeley had two conditions: first, I was to conduct all research necessary to ensure that all facts in the book were accurate. That meant every town and city name needed to be confirmed since so many of the places in my mother's memoir had entirely different names prior to the Nazi occupation of Eastern Europe. Next, I was asked to rewrite the manuscript.

I was also asked to enrich the chapters, adding accurate details about the time period and the various settings. That included descriptions about scenery, towns, ethnic foods, vegetation, housing styles, social and cultural standards—in fact, there were so many details I had to get right but I had no clue where to begin!

Up to that point I'd been completing my PhD dissertation. It was my good fortune that the one skill I really mastered while at the University of Chicago was research methodology. But the big drawback was that I'd never before done research of this kind. I applied my academic research skills to searching for the many details I'd need about life in Eastern Europe during the early 1900's and up to the end of World War II. It was surprisingly difficult and time-consuming. I muddled my way through it, learning as I went along. Exactly where should I look for the information? That was my biggest roadblock. At that point I consulted the university's reference librarians, spoke with numerous historical experts, interviewed professors who taught military courses and who had themselves been in the military, and even asked those who taught classes in Slavic Studies or Jewish Studies for reference suggestions.

Gradually, I compiled a body of reliable reference books and sources of my own. And gradually, I acquired not only a good understanding of the process but also an intense appreciation for the kinds of details critical to establishing credibility in writing scenes about time and place. So many of us forget that all stories, whether fiction or non-fiction, occur in a setting composed of time and place.

I began revisiting my own short stories and essays, rethinking the importance of details – where and how writers find them and especially the importance of reliability and accuracy. Once I began teaching writing workshops, It became clear that this part of writing – the research process, presents a daunting challenge to most writers. I handed out copies of my brief bibliography to my classes, all of which were filled with accomplished writers.

Over the years, my list of bibliographical sources has increased steadily. Dependence on internet research also has increased, but identifying accurate information online has become very time-consuming. It can be frustrating , and new concerns about reliability of information obtained online have been increasing.

In this book, I share my research experiences, resources, and observations at a time when internet sources are being over-used and hardcopy references and other real-life sources are being abandoned. In my bibliography I also convey the importance of references beyond those available online. Once you begin conducting research by consulting some of the sources in this book, you'll begin to wonder why you haven't done more hard-copy and situational research.

Get the facts, or the facts will get you. And when you get them, get them right, or they will get you wrong.

Dr. Thomas Fuller (1654 - 1734), Gnomologia, 1732

Facts do not cease to exist because they are ignored.

-Aldous Huxley (1894 -1963), "Proper Studies," 1927

Introduction

The current era is an incredibly challenging and exciting time in which to be both a writer and a researcher. First, to be a writer, one must also be a researcher. Tough to imagine honest writing without honest, accurate and reliable information so it follows that top quality research is a must for every writer.

The range of available references dealing with topic-specific information really has become near limitless. If we include internet-accessible sites such as: online encyclopedias and reference materials, websites maintained by countless academic institutions, and others hosted by governmental agencies—all publicly accessible, surely the magnitude becomes overwhelming. While most of these are relatively easy to access, determining which ones contain reliable information is surprisingly time-consuming, challenging and insanely frustrating. And that's exactly my point!

All this easy access we have to the unimaginable quantities of information available online, combined with the convenience of carrying out serious research dependent upon internet sources, diminishes our understanding of just how critically important hardcopy sources continue to be. My key position: the world of tangible sources such as books, journals, atlases, newspapers, public records, even "in-person" interviews, shouldn't be disregarded simply because internet research strikes so many of us as much faster, less laborious and a convenient approach that can be carried out from almost anywhere on the planet.

Books and documents that are accessible only by visiting libraries, books stores, museums and public archives are becoming increasingly under-utilized. Further, an entire array of printed materials—not of the library or bookstore variety, but rather those found in a wide range of places, also are incredibly valuable to establishing credibility in our writing. And finally, two other critical bodies of documentation, not in print at all, but available in our real world (as opposed to a virtual one) so many writers overlook are:

1. In-person interviews, whether conducted with experts as original research or as a secondary data source gleaned from audio recordings or interviews offer valuable avenues for information gathering;

2. Personal visits to physical locations, those about which we're writing, also are an important part of what I regard as real-life experiential research.

Now, I've added an interesting example about experiential research. Some authors have gone so far as attempting to experience some of the events about which they've written. As with all things, there are—of course, extremes to the experiential approach. One of my favorite examples was described in a Wall Street Journal article I read (Books section) dated May 23, 2013. The heading was as follows; "Philipp Meyer: An Obsessed Novelist's Extreme Research."

I was intrigued and drawn in by my desire to understand exactly what might constitute the process referred to as "extreme research." Mr. Meyer's novel, *The Son*, contains a scene in which a boy is captured by Comanche Indians. The boy must eat bloody raw buffalo liver, a test he must pass and one that for him and his captors will mean the difference between his life and death.

The author, in his pledge to write accurately about events of the period, takes his research to an entirely new level. His approach is a gigantic step beyond the academic and certainly galaxies beyond the internet. Mr. Meyer travels to a ranch in Texas where he shoots two buffalo. He then proceeds to drink a mug full of blood— an experience the author describes as utterly revolting but one he was convinced was critical to his being able to write both accurately, as well as intensely, about the main character's reactions. Hard to imagine anything even close to this kind of research being done via internet sites!

There are less extreme experiential research approaches but those, too, bypass the internet. They depend upon travel and "in-person" experiences. Writing about nonfiction historical events, family histories, and memoirs demands accurate knowledge about very specific places and times. One fail-proof way in which to enrich and validate the content of such work is to visit these very places. Not much can be done about traveling back into the past —at least not in the present era, but placing ourselves on-location can benefit our historical research, positioning us to find help from local experts.

One of my favorite books in which so much of the author's time and energy was devoted to the research, particularly by visiting all the locations in which her story occurs, is entitled *Blood Work: A Tale of Medicine and Murder in the Scientific Revolution* by science writer, Holly Tucker. In her effort to describe accurately and realistically the sounds, scents and visual surround of 17th-century London and Paris, Ms. Tucker travels to both cities. Once there, she wanders through the streets and neighborhoods – the actual settings where much of this true story occurred.

Beyond that, Ms. Tucker sought out architectural libraries with their historical documents and drawings, city planning maps, business records, and even health records. She consulted with transportation experts plus a wide range of authorities and academics, all to help her recreate accurate, multi-sensory descriptions of these seventeenth century cities.

So Just What Is the Problem?

So what's the problem with online or virtual research you might ask? Well, vastly more than you could imagine at first glance, so read on!

Many writers in my research workshops have stumbled upon the answer to that seemingly mindless question the hard way. Consider, for instance, that almost all facts and information you'll locate online (and likely will use) to support and enhance your writing is as reliable or credible as is the quality of internet sources you've decided to access.

Remember, public, free on-line encyclopedias vary widely both in their degrees of accuracy and in their reliability levels. In fact, even within the exact same online encyclopedias, accuracy of the individual posts varies. Why? Obvious – the quality of any post is completely dependent upon the diligence and capabilities of individual researchers and contributors.

Google searches and *Wikipedia* entries do yield tremendous amounts of information–all of which we'd love to assume is accurate. If it were in fact so, then that certainly would make writers' jobs of conducting research and collecting data so much faster and definitely much easier. But truthfully, a fair portion of the information collected online does require further validation. That process is best accomplished through additional systematic academic research.

What do I mean by this? Simple. Not all types of research can or should be carried out via the virtual world of on-line. Consulting hard-copy materials, real-life experts who might be amenable to being interviewed, documents and historical data, and even seeking advice from professional reference librarians still prove tough-to-replace resources.

"Real world" serious, academic caliber research continues to lend an air of detail and credibility to all writing that otherwise might be near impossible to replicate. Besides all this, you'll be building an accurate and reliable bibliography for your own future research as well as one that may benefit your readers.

What's the bottom line of all this? Answer: learn how to conduct "off-line" research, where to go for the specific types of data you need, and how to use it and you'll benefit tremendously. Credibility and accuracy of the details in your writing can only benefit its quality, simultaneously enhancing your "writerly" reputation—a great sequence.

What's the Focus?

My recommendations are geared to writers who need (or want) to understand very specific aspects and facts of history, culture, various sciences, geography, economics, research methods and even memoir writing strategies in order to be able to present details skillfully and accurately in their writing. Most of the references included in my list are exactly the same ones I've used consistently during the past few years. In fact, I continue to rely upon them often but beyond these, I've also consulted sources I hadn't been aware existed until I scanned bibliographies of the books I had been using.

It was in those bibliographies where I learned of so many other exceptionally well documented reliable references. Where ever possible, I've written brief summary descriptions about my recommended sources. These appear, for instance, following any reference about which I have either in-depth knowledge or strong opinions.

I've focused almost all of my attention on hard-copy material plus in-person research efforts. Those few on-line sources included have been placed at the end of my bibliographical categories. I faced a great deal of back-and-forth questioning: do I restrict my recommendations to hard-copy plus in-person references or should I include online sources?

It became obvious that adding some websites made good research sense given one major qualifier; no hard-copy versions of these decidedly specialized resources exist nor have they existed. Those I've added came into operation as the internet evolved into a user-friendly, research supportive medium. Consequently, websites included here are regarded as very reputable.

You might be wondering, "Like what?" One perfect example is the website *ancestry.com* that provides valuable information and resources to writers looking for genealogical facts. Another is the familysearch.com project. And in addition to these, several other highly reliable sites include those maintained by the Library of Congress (*loc.gov/index.html*), the Franklin D. Roosevelt Presidential Museum (*fdrlibrary.marist.edu/*), and the United States Holocaust Memorial Museum (*ushmm.org/*).

My decision to add these, plus a few others was simply a judgment call but, more than anything else, was fueled by my own past experiences of spending way too much time and effort searching for accurate, supportive information online.

Acknowledging Change

As writers, we should remind ourselves constantly that a huge chunk of historical and scientific information is anything but static. New evidence always surfaces; scientific theories are being disproven on a regular basis; secondary sources such as personal journals, letters and public documents occasionally are revealed as inaccurate or too subjective to be considered entirely factual. These types of events exemplify that information exists in a state of constant flux—changing continuously as both technology and time demand that we re-evaluate, re-examine and revise our theories. We might want to consider that the information we think of as "facts" ought to be referred to as "currently held beliefs."

This all points to one important problem: available modern references that cite specific discoveries, theories and facts may–in a single moment's notice, become obsolete. I'm thinking about news making discoveries as a good example of such a scenario. Imagine, for instance, that a previously unknown painting by an old master surfaces; a newly found letter written by a president 100 years ago proves significant enough to alter contemporary opinions; or on a more personal level—we discover genealogical evidence that has great bearing upon our own life's stories.

A Last Note

I've limited the number of "coffee table books" and mass market general fact books included in my research bibliography. Even so, there still are a few important "stand-bys" I simply couldn't bring myself to exclude. Regarding some of my summaries, I selected sources based upon publishers' reviews and after using those very sources myself, added to publishers' notes—both positive and negative.

The sky is not less blue because the blind man does not see it.

-Danish proverb

Carelessness is worse than a thief.

-Scottish Proverb

I

General References & Research Sources

We've all used general, readily available reference books, the kind found at most libraries. Many of these sources are long time standards, for example: encyclopedias, dictionaries, and atlases. A wide range of these, while readily available, aren't particularly well known even though they offer excellent information. Based on my experience, this list contains highly reliable sources.

American Reference Books Annual 2010, Vol.41.
Shannon Graff Hysell, Associate Editor. 2010.
Libraries Unlimited.

This is a reference book for reference books. The most recently published edition lists high-quality materials accompanied by critical reviews. More than 1,500 reviews of print resources and online references have been written by more than 400 academic, public, and school librarians. All the contributors are regarded as experts in their fields. Approximately 500 subjects are covered in disciplines that include social sciences, humanities, science and technology.

<u>Bartlett's Familiar Quotations: A Collection of Passages, Phrases, and Proverbs Traced to Their Sources in Ancient and Modern Literature</u>, (17th edition).

Bartlett, John, and Justin Kaplan, Editor. 2002. Little Brown and Co., Boston, MA.

Started in 1855 and continuously updated, Bartlett's is a "must-have" very reliable collection of phrases, passages, and proverbs that lists original sources. In addition, all citations are cross-referenced by topic and source.

<u>The Address Book: How To Reach Anyone Who Is Anyone</u>, (8th edition). Levine, Michael. 1997. Berkley Group, New York, NY.

Yes—this, too, is dated by current standards but it does contain excellent suggestions that continue to be reliable, helpful and accurate. It's self-explanatory, but due to tremendous changes in the internet, a new version would undeniably be a big help.

<u>The Oxford Guide to Library Research</u>.

Mann, Thomas. 2005. Oxford University Press, New York.

This one is definitely my favorite guide of all time. It's becoming increasingly difficult—if not impossible, to be a respectable writer without also being a proficient (okay, a really good) researcher. Now, because of the quantities of available information combined with complexity of retrieval, any writer conducting research will benefit from aquiring a clear, comprehensive understanding of his or her information retrieval options.

The third edition of *The Oxford Guide to Library Research* includes both print and online approaches to conducting research, but a really nice quality of Mann's guide, is his inclusion of specific search techniques that can be applied to almost any research field.

Mann definitely is a man after my own heart! (Pun?) He elaborates about the reasons our opportunities and abilities to browse library shelves remain critically important even in the present-day on-line, computer age. The author shows us the timeless importance of physical libraries, books, and more traditional research methods. Better yet, he still includes some helpful advice about online research.

I really appreciate that Dr. Mann included examples from his own experiences conducting research plus from the work he's done assisting others in their research on a wide range of topics. If I were deciding to purchase only one general research guide, *The Oxford Guide to Library Research* ranks at the top of my list.

Sociology – A Guide To Reference and Information Sources, (3rd edition). Aby, Stephen H. 2005. Libraries Unlimited, Englewood, CO.

In world Filled with "references to references," this is one of them. *Sociology – A Guide To Reference and Information Sources* summarizes 610 primary sociology sources in addition to those in the related social sciences. The emphasis is upon works published in the United States, Great Britain, Canada and Australia from 1997 through early 2004.

The New York Times Guide to Essential Knowledge: Completely Revised and Expanded, (2nd Edition).
(Multiple editors and contributors). 2007.
St. Martin's Press, New York, NY.

Organized by broad categories, this guide includes arts, economics, business and finance, science and technology, sports, nations and even origins of the world's languages. Categories are subdivided further, for example: art is comprised of film, visual arts, music and the performing arts. It's a very handy reference source for quick fact-checking or information.

The Sourcebook to Public Record Information: The Comprehensive Guide to County, State and Federal Public Records Sources.
Weber, Peter J., and Michael Sankey, Editors. 2008.
BRB Publications, Portland, OR.

Any writer needing information contained in public records needs to consult this guide. The real attraction: any writer who has ever attempted to conduct research requiring public record information knows how totally "crazy-making" that process can be. *The Sourcebook to Public Record Information* begins with an instructional approach, explaining exactly how to find and use public records.

The sources listed include federal records that "live" in physical settings plus many newly available online. This sourcebook is especially helpful for anyone interested in these types of records for purposes of legal research, background investigations, screenings, locating people or assets, or in order to gather genealogy data.

Organized by state, every chapter contains helpful telephone numbers—one feature that's incredibly useful, plus contact information lists identifying specifics requirements that must be met in order to gain access to records at different of levels. What's included? State agencies, state licensing boards, federal courts, county or regional courts, and recording bureaus.

The new edition has 96 additional pages that contain updated telephone numbers and new internet accessible sites, state maps and new (but limited) information about Canadian records. The only difficulty I found with this reference is that it's missing an index. Really strange! Other than that one glitch, it's an excellent source book.

The most successful man
in life is the man who has
the best information.

-Benjamin Disraeli

II

Society and Culture

The Dictionary of All Scriptures and Myths.
Gaskell, G.A. 1960. The Julian Press, Inc., Crown
Publishers. New York, N.Y.

This dictionary is a definitive and comprehensive study of definitions and terms associated with all world religions plus their related myths. A real tome logging in at 842 pages, it's a compilation of the particulars and historical records about modern day organized religions, primitive religious practices, beliefs, and mythology.

Handbook of Christian Feasts and Customs.
Weiser, Francis X. 1952. Hartcourt-Brace & Worldwide,
Inc., NY.

This one is incredibly dated but even so, it continues to be helpful and tough to substitute. Could this be an indication of an absence of significant changes to a host of organized religions during the last six decades? The handbook is a wonderfully detailed history packed with information about feasts, customs, holydays and holidays of the Christian liturgical year. There's even a fun section–well, fun for this type of text that is. How about details and interesting facts about folklore?

20,000 Years of Fashion: the History of Costume and Personal Adornment, (Expanded Edition).
Boucher, Francois. 1987.
Harry N. Abrams, Inc., New York, NY.

This amazingly comprehensive history of costumes and adornment is indispensable to anyone writing about topics that include descriptions about people—their cultures and hence, their clothing.

The Greenwood Encyclopedia of Clothing through World History, (3 Volumes).
Condra, Jill. 2007. Greenwood Press, Santa Barbara, CA.

Reviewing this book has given me a new appreciation for the terrifically important role accurate details related to fashion and clothing plays in correctly positioning characters in time and place. This encyclopedia has had a substantial effect on how much attention I now pay to characters' wardrobes when I watch period movies. I'm sure that even a quick review of this reference will do the same for you.

Articles in this encyclopedia were written by a wide

range of experts. The emphasis is on the history of clothing and textiles ending in the year 2006 and spanning world cultures. The specialties and research interests include forensic archaeology, art and art history, classics, fashion history, ancient religion and medicine, fashion design, plus costume design. Each of the three volumes contains approximately 400 items and includes a first-rate bibliography of additional books, websites, and films that might be useful to those conducting further research.

One reviewer noted, "The set succeeds remarkably well in placing clothing in its historical and social context. Researchers can turn to this set first for the most essential information about a time, place, and style of dress." My own opinion is that *The Greenwood Encyclopedia is* comprehensive and marvelously engaging.

The Encyclopedia of Money.
Allen, Larry. 1999. ABC-CLIO Publishing,
Santa Barbara, CA.

This is the true story of money, barter and various media of exchange that contains detailed information about the currencies of all nations. In addition to extensive historical notes, there are numerous photographs. A useful bibliographical index lists additional sources, while the table of contents is nicely organized and cross-referenced by country. It's very useful to anyone writing about foreign events.

The Food Encyclopedia: Ingredients, Tools, Techniques, and People.
Rolland, Jacques L., and Carol Sherman. 2006. Robert Rose, Inc., Toronto, Ontario, Canada.

The Food Encyclopedia is true to its title. The Authors present historical and cultural food-related definitions that are organized alphabetically and cross-referenced. The text includes exceptional illustrations. Especially appealling, the book is written in an easy to read, non-technical style, providing extensive information about all matters "food." Included: geographic origins, uses, common names, variations by nationalities plus biographical notes to help readers with further research.

Crimes and Punishments: The Illustrated Crime Encyclopedia. (Multiple volumes 1-28).
H.S. Stutman, Inc., Publishers. Westport, CT.

Crimes, criminals, methods and means by which they were captured—these are the primary topics detailed in *Crimes and Punishment*. This comprehensive reference source combines a huge range of information compiled from data contained in police records and court murder casebooks plus from issues in the science of criminology and legal matters. It's helpful to writers of fiction and nonfiction alike and can be a great device for setting time and place.

Great American Trials: From Salem Witchcraft to Rodney King.

Knappman, Edward W., Editor. 1995. Invisible Ink Press,

All essays—whether nonfiction or fiction, demand that the writer establishes convincing time or historical settings. We all agree that stories are set within the context of place and time. It follows that one of the most convincing, relevant ways to establish believability this is by placing stories and characters within the context of top news events of the era. Trials are often neglected as worthwhile, important, and credible historical markers.

Another consideration is that levels of media attention and reportage afforded to trials reflect society's values and mores during the years of given trials. A good example is Brown vs. Board of Education, set in 1954. By considering the issues and events of the case, we can gain excellent insight into the volatility of race relations in America at that time.

Some additional well known trials to think about include: The Scopes Monkey Trial set in 1925; Patty Hearst Trial (1976); John Demjanjuk Denaturalization Trial (1981); Mapplethorpe Obscenity Trial (1990); William Kennedy Smith Trial (1991); Police Officers Accused of Violating Rodney King's Civil Rights (1993).

The glossary and index are well-organized, but because the collection is so absorbing, I'd suggest avoiding it unless you have a good deal of time to leaf through it.

Best Loved Songs of the American People.
Agay, Denes. 1975. Double Day and Company, New York, NY.

Organized by titles and by era, this song reference includes helpful and fun historical notes. It also contains sheet music. I found that pretty amazing. This is a perfect resource for establishing time-setting particularly for memoir writers.

The Guinness Encyclopedia of Popular Music.
(Multiple volumes). Larkin, Colin, Editor. 1995. Guinness Publishing, Stockton Press, New York, NY.

Guinness books generally tend to be easy to use. This one is no exception. *The Encyclopedia of Popular Music,* spread across multiple volumes, is also relatively easy to use primarily owing to its logically organized format. Information is cross-referenced by performers, group names, and song writers.

It also includes major song titles, their dates, top albums plus fun information about the artists' colleagues during their own eras, their influences, and even helpful historical notes about entertainment.

The New Grove Dictionary of Music and Musicians.
(Multiple volumes).
Sadie, Stanly, Editor. 2004. Oxford University Press, New York, NY.

This dictionary is a nice reference for the writer who needs to (or wants to) add accurate details about music to their work as an approach to enhance the time-setting of content. Included are several fun photographs—not nearly enough as far as I'm concerned, illustrations, historical references, and information specific to international music and musicians not to be found in most references of this type. The bibliography is extensive and in it I found additional worthwhile sources.

Atlas of Human Migration.

Russell King, Editor. 2007. Firefly Books, LTD., Buffalo, NY.

This atlas was a lucky find! Why? Because it details all major mass migrations throughout time, and across cultures, plus presents absorbing assessments of their causes and effects. In addition, traditional migrations' routes are identified.

Summaries of historical contexts provide wonderful perspective aimed at improving our understanding of these major migratory events. Some examples: American colonization, slaves and convicts, industrializations, famines, wars and persecutions. The volume contains plentiful photographs, excellent maps, and highly useful timelines.

Research serves to make building stones out of stumbling blocks.

-Arthur D. Little

III

Geography and Places

<u>Encyclopedia of Urban America – The Cities and Suburbs,</u>
(2 Volumes).
Neil Larry Shumsky, Editor. 1998. ABC-CLIO Publishing,
Oxford, England.

Encyclopedia of Urban America contains more than 500 entries with details about numerous important topics; major cities, suburbs, people, places, concepts, contemporary issues, history and development of urban America. The discussion encompasses problems associated with both urban and suburban areas. Issues are as diverse as crime, pollution, congestion, the arts and humanities, social issues, religion, infrastructure, noteworthy individuals, and economics.

This encyclopedia includes plenty of illustrations, photographs, and maps as well as cross-references to all information and various bibliographies. The index is nicely organized too—all combining to make this an easy book to use. The greatest drawback is that, like too many other references of this type, information tends to be very out-dated. Writers using this resource would be wise to double check more currently available demographic records.

Almanac of the 50 States 2010: Comparative Data Profiles & Guide to Government Data. Corporate Authors. 2010. Information Publications, Palo Alto, CA.

Almanac of the 50 States is the comprehensive clearinghouse for extensive data about all 50 states plus the District of Columbia. That alone is enough to make it an incredibly helpful reference source. It's been referred to as the essential research tool for anyone conducting research or seeking specific facts about the United States.

My own experience with it has been positive, confirming that it's highly usable, primarily because it's so well-organized. As a result, it's helpful to researchers at almost any level. Although compact, it contains plenty of information about every state for anyone needing demographic information, analysis and research.

This almanac is great for quick fact-finding about very specific items such as; state bird, major industry, crime rates, population, mean incomes, and even political participation.

Don't Know Much About Geography: Everything You Needed to Know About the World But Never Learned. David, Kenneth C. 2004. Perennial-Harper Collins Publishers, New York, NY.

My comments: exactly the same as for Mr. David's book entitled, *Don't Know Much About History*. Simply substitute "geography" with the word "history" and you've got it! That, however, doesn't make it any less valuable as a reference tool.

The 50 States of the United States Capital and Information Links.

The reference is one comprised of mostly actual information about geographic locations, state birds, colleges and universities, constitutions, indigenous flowers, genealogical resources, geological formations, geographical features, mottos, national forests and parks, newspapers, nicknames, nonprofit organizations, populations, state and federal representatives, songs, and the dates of entry into the union. Very basic, factual, and updated regularly.

The World Factbook 2013-14.
The Central Intelligence Agency, 2013. Publisher:
The Central Intelligence Agency, Washington, DC.

Incredibly comprehensive, *The World Factbook* contains information and statistics about more than 250 countries plus other entities. These data are collected and produced by the US Central Intelligence Agency. The fact that it's updated annually makes it a real stand-out, especially since so many fact books and references are updated too infrequently to make them indispensable.

Regional Landscapes of the United States and Canada.
Stephen S. Birdsall. 1992. John Wiley Press,
New York, NY.

There's not much to say about this reference other than the obvious, plus how much fun it is to look at. It can provide some details additional detail to writers needing to add information about geography in their work.

Data is what distinguishes the dilettante from the artist.

-George V. Higgins

With so much information now online, it is exceptionally easy to simply dive in and drown.

-Alfred Glossbrenner

IV

Historical References

Don't Know Much About History: Everything You Needed to Know About American History But Never Learned.
David, Kenneth C. 2003. Perennial-Harper Collins Publishers, New York, NY.

A clear, accessible guide perfect for fact-checking. I think the title really says it all.

Great Events From History – American Series.
Loos, L., and Frank N. Magill, Editors. Salem Press, Inc., Englewood Cliffs, NJ.

Hard to believe but, exactly one thousand historical events are detailed in this easy-to-read summary form. The publication consists of multiple volumes and includes a table of contents filled with dates, major events, and good suggestions for further readings. It's especially helpful for easy fact/date checking.

The Holocaust Encyclopedia.
Laquer, Walter, ed. Baumel, Judith T. 2001. Yale University Press, New haven, CT.

Oxford Encyclopedia of Women in World History,
(Multiple volumes).
Editor: Smith, Bonnie G. 2008. Oxford University Press, New York, NY.

A comprehensive topical outline of entries organized alphabetically, this encyclopedia focuses entirely upon women. Also included are bibliographical references following every entry as a suggestion for further research.

Atlas of World History.
O'Brien, Patrick K., Editor. 1999. Oxford University Press, New York, NY.

Spark Charts: U.S. History 1492-1865. Barnes & Noble Publishing, Inc.

Spark Charts: U.S. History 1865-2004. Barnes & Noble Publishing, Inc.

These charts are triple-folded and plastic laminated. They present in grid format historical events, dates, and summary paragraphs. Their indestructible design is great for writers who need quick, accessible information often.

Not having the information you need
when you need it leaves you wanting.
Not knowing where to look for that
information leaves you powerless.
In a society where information is
king, none of us can afford that.

-Lois Horowi

I find that a great part of the information I have, was acquired by looking up something and finding something else on the way.

-Franklin Pierce Adam

V

Almanacs

Just what is an almanac and what makes it different from other reference books? An almanac, by definition, predicts and records astronomical events, for instance: sun rise and sun set times, full moons, anticipated sea levels and days of tides, weather, and other factors directly related to time. In more recent years, almanacs have been expanded to include a wide range of information categories. Additions are: culture and society, recipes, and even gardening hints. The main characteristic of an almanac is that the information is perceived to be reliable, plus the style is factual, practical and totally unembellished.

According to the *2010 Random House-Kernerman Webster's College Dictionary* definition, "an almanac is a publication containing astronomical and meteorological information." Some of these are the predicted future positions of celestial objects, star magnitudes, and positions of major star constellations.

The Old Farmer's Almanac is one of the earliest of this type of book compiled and published in the United States—starting in 1792. Originally, it's focus was true to it's title. The information dealt with farmers' needs plus aspects of weather and astronomy that were deemed to have a potential impact upon both crop planting and harvesting times, food preservation techniques, recipes, and numerous practical health and survival tips.

The modern category entitled "almanacs" has evolved and now includes any annual reference book of facts. Guinness was the first of these. They began to compile and publish topic-specific almanacs such as: sports, entertainment, world records and numerous other fields.

Baseball Almanac. The Baseball Maniac's Almanac: The Absolutely, Positively, and Without Question Greatest Book of Facts, Figures, and Astonishing Lists Ever Compiled, (Third edition).
Sugar, Bert Randolph and Staurt Shea. 2012.
Sports Publishing; McGraw-Hill, New York, NY.

This truly is about baseball and only about baseball. It's absolutely everything baseball from history, to players' and owners' biographies, chronologies, important statistics, information concerning baseball collectibles, analysis about important games, teams, reviews about films, even baseball related songs and poetry. All that's missing is peanuts and Cracker Jack™.

The Almanac of American Politics -2010.
Michael Barone, Richard E. Cohen, and Jackie Koszczuk, Editors. 2011. University of Chicago Press, Chicago, IL.

The last edition of the *Almanac of American Politics* published focuses upon politics in the year 2014 with the release date September 2013. A comprehensive political reference guide, this almanac contains profiles of every member of Congress and the governor of each state. It also presents in-depth discussions about the politics of each of the states plus every House district. The Alamanc is comprised of twenty volumes. An updated issue is published every two years.

The Old Farmer's Almanac 2013.
Old Farmer's Almanac (Author). 2013. Old Farmer's Almanac Publishing.

This classic, started in 1792, has long been regarded as the essential reference source by the reviewers in *Choice & American Reference Books Annual*. *Old Farmer's* perfectly exemplifies the definition and description of "almanac" I presented at the beginning of this section.

Guinness World Records - Home of the Longest, Shortest, Fastest.
Guinness World Records NA, Inc., New York, NY.

The ultimate authority on record-breaking achievements, Guinness Books are published annually in numerous fact book categories that can be purchased at book stores (remember those?) ordered online at the following sites:

Records:

www.guinnessworldrecords.com/records

Human Body:

www.guinnessworldrecords.com/records/humanbody/

Guinness World Records 2010:

www.Guinnessworldrecords.com/es

Sports & Games

www.guinnessworldrecords.com/records/sportsand_games

Amazing Feats

www.guinnessworldrecords.com/records/amazing_feats

Natural World

www.guinnessworldrecords.com/records/natural_world

A half truth is a whole lie.

-Yiddish Proverb

Research is to see what everybody else has seen and to think what nobody else has thought.

Albert Szent-Gyorgyi (1893 - 1986)

VI

Guns, Bombs, and Bullets

Information about weaponry and the military is grouped together in this reference category. Even though most of the references that follow are historical, the list is a good starting point.

American Military History: A Guide to Reference and Information Services, (Second Edition).
> Blewett, Daniel K. 2008. Libraries Unlimited Publishers.

A Civilian's Guide to the U.S. Military: A Comprehensive Reference to the Customs, Language and Structure of the Armed Forces.
> Schading, Barbara and Richard Schading. 2006 Writer's Digest Books, F+W Media Inc., New York, NY.

Confused about military terms? If so, this is a reference book to help straighten you out, especially if you're having difficulty with acronyms, equipment, and protocol being discussed.

The authors have done a super job clarifying information as it pertains to each military branch: Army, Navy, Marines,   Air Force, and even the Coast Guard. The book includes an easy-to-read chart of rank, associated insignias, plus very consice explanations of each branch's organizational structure. Now I can listen to enthusiasts discussing military events and exhibit a bit more comprehension. If I can grasp these structures, it's possible that one day I'll comprehend American football.

Essential Militaria: Facts, Legends and Curiosities About Warfare Through the Ages.
Hobbes, Nicholas. 2003. Grove Atlantic, Inc.,
New York, NY.

The Gun Digest Book of Combat Handgunnery.
Ayoob, Massad. 2007. Gun Digest Books.

Complete Book Of Combat Handgunning.
Taylor, Chuck. 1981. Paladin Press. Boulder, CO.

Pistols of the World – 4th Edition.
Hogg, Ian V. and John Walter. 2004. David and Charles.

The West Point Atlas of American Wars.
Esposito, Vincent J. 1995. United States Military Academy, Henry Holt & Company.

The 1995 edition is the most recent one, revised and updated. It's the definitive atlas of all wars and every major conflict (from 1869 to 1900) in which the United States was involved. There are even details about the Revolutionary War, War of 1812, and Civil War. *The West Point Atlas* was out of print for almost a decade. Once it was reissued, The Boston Herald cited it as, "A work of tremendous importance…a brilliantly concise and lucid history of each war."

The atlas actually consists of two volumes; the first - about colonial fighting in North America through the Spanish-American War, places heavy emphasis upon the Civil War. The second volume focuses on World Wars I and II.

Included also are highly-detailed maps accompanied by descriptions of campaigns and battles in which American troops and naval units were involved. It presents views of the wars from various generals' perspectives, descriptions of strategies employed to achieve victories, details about infrastructure essential for protection, difficult logistics, and more information about outcomes of their decisions.

The maps range from national scope to very local—detailing rivers, roads, railroads, and hills that played crucial roles in the outcome of every battle.

Get your facts first, and then you can distort them as much as you please.

-Mark Twain. American humorist, novelist, author

VII

Sciences and Associated Technical References

Just how do you gain access to top quality technical references? Can you find them at a local public library? Usually not – that is, not unless you're located in a large city that supports a university, or two or three or if you live in a university town. Local, public libraries generally focus on providing services assumed to meet their communities' particular interests. And those services always seem concentrated on business, history, social issues, entertainment, and school projects.

The majority of science references held at local libraries are aimed at readers with a science education level of between junior-high to high-school. Consequently, these libraries don't include text books or highly technical references. Their readership numbers simply are way too low for these libraries to invest in such highly specialized collections. Besides, high level references almost always consist of multiple volumes. Because of that, they also consume valuable shelf space that otherwise could be used more effectively to accommodate different materials – ones that will serve a broader readership.

Lower level science books, while certainly adequate for lay-readers, definitely are not advanced enough to meet the needs of technical readers, science readers, and writers who need to understand the finer details of particular disciplines. By the way, it's not always just science writers who search for technical information. Responsible writers whose works contain any kind of technical or scientific terms and information depend heavily upon these types of references to validate their own content.

Given such constraints, what are the best ways in which to gain access to specialized references I've reviewed here? Try my four fool-proof—or almost fool-proof approaches.

1. Obtain access to a private technical library

Many exist – often in some unlikely places. Several come to mind immediately, such as collections maintained by organizations, associations, technical schools, even withen corporations that produce related technical products. By making some preliminary phone calls, researchers usually can gain access even if they can't necessarily obtain borrowing privileges. Besides that, remember copying equipment is almost always available at these locations, providing an alternative to borrowing.

2. Travel to a university library known to have an extensive reference collection

Conducting preliminary research about regional universities' libraries and their specialized holdings, will help you identify those most suited to meeting your specific research needs. Depending upon how extensive your research needs are, it's often possible to schedule appointments with reference librarians who can provide insight into the process and suggest additional reference avenues.

3. Purchase the reference yourself

This approach isn't necessarily the most economical one but it may be well worth the investment. It's a decision you can make only if you take into account that, if the reference is one you'll be using extensively then purchasing provides a great convenience. Besides, consider the savings you'll realize by eliminating repeat visits to libraries or book stores and omitting copying costs.

Second, many highly specialized reference materials have very robust secondary markets. I've actually experienced two situations in which I resold reference books for more than I paid to purchase them. And that leads to my next suggestion; many highly specialized technical references can be purchased inexpensively on the secondary market, from on-line booksellers as well as university and college bookstores.

4. Borrow specialized references

It might just be possible to identify independent professionals, experts, professors or friends whose interests include the technical area in which you're conducting research. This takes a bit of doing, a bit of self confidence, and maybe even some asking around, but some of these individuals may be willing to lend out selections from their own collections.

Some Facts About Borrowing and Purchasing

Libraries that do maintain adequate collections, i.e., private technical libraries and university libraries, rarely lend out their references, neither do they allow materials to be removed from their reference rooms. In most libraries, you must read references on-site and take notes or—as in most cases, make copies. The problem is that few of us can read, conduct research, take notes, and write all at the same time.

What exactly was behind this statement? It's just advisory. Be prepared to devote a good chunk of time to the research phase of your writing. The process yields the best results when not rushed and done systematically. Consider copying segments of references you need but also purchasing a copy-card will help reduce the per-copy price.

If you do choose to purchase your references, most can be special-ordered through science book clubs or through general-interest independent bookstores. Prices always will vary depending upon where you purchase and how long the book has been in print.

Occasionally, I receive discount offers for orders I place through specific independent bookstores. And sure, some large chains or online bookstores might offer 10% discounts on "all hardcovers," but for some reason, they're rarley applicable to specialized science or technical books and seem never to apply to orders I've placed. Maybe you'll have better luck with this.

Science book-clubs offer discounts that may not seem like any big deal but when you consider that technical and specialized references can cost well over $150, the discounts are well worth the effort. Science book-clubs generally provide reviews about their references often indicating which have been well-received by researchers and professionals in those fields. The Library of Science compiles expensive lists of titles that include suggested texts for writers. The remaining titles that follow are science and technical references.

General Science

Science News -Weekly News Magazine,
Published by Science Service.

Particularly well-written, this science magazine is a highly regarded publication for science-oriented lay-readers. Even though familiarity with biology, genetics, chemistry, physics, astronomy, and statistical analysis is recommended, it's not crucial. The publication is helpful for writers of science fiction, mainstream, and thrillers.

Science News is a good source for keeping them current about general research and development, for provoking ideas and directing writers to new references for highly specialized information.

Published as a weekly magazine containing reviews about recent discoveries plus new research in all scientific disciplines. Each issue has two feature articles that focus upon recently researched problems. Some examples of past articles: creating microscopic light-emitting patterns on the surface of silicon crystal, Hubble telescope updates and discoveries, the coldest star discovered to date, kidney stones and beverages, rotaviruses, chlorophyll eyes in fish, fungi and old books, fetal deaths correlated with air pollution and odd heartbeats.

Most of the overviews in *Science News Weekly* correspond to articles published in newspapers and in *Nature, Science*, plus numerous major scientific journals.

Stedman's Medical Dictionary, (25th Edition).
William R. Hensyl, Harriet Felscher, and Bill Cady, Editors. 1990. Williams and Wilkins.

Stedman's includes an excellent sub-entry locator plus a brief medical etymology. Some background in biology and a basic knowledge about medical procedures would be useful. Writers dealing with medical conditions such as diseases, injury, trauma or death would be wise to own a copy of this dictionary to supplement other references.

Color Atlas of Anatomy, (2nd Edition).
McMinn, Hutchings, Pegington, and Abrahams, Editors. 1988. Mosby-Wolfe Publishers.

This is a valuable anatomical reference filled with clear, detailed photographs but beyond that, it's also good fun to look at. Background in biology, medical terms, and medical procedures could be helpful. After looking at it carefully myself, it could work as a good reference for anyone writing science fiction, mystery, fantasy, and thrillers. This atlas is especially helpful when writing anything that includes discussions of injury, trauma, or death. *Color Atlas of Anatomy* is a good general reference about muscles, bones, and organs.

Organizationally, it's well thought out. The sections group together head, neck, and brain; vertebral column and spinal cord; upper limb; thorax; abdomen and pelvis; and lower limb. Besides the photographs, it contains x-rays and drawings that help illustrate body parts such as membranes and venous paths. Included is an index to arteries, veins, nerves, lymphatic system.

Field's Virology - 4th Edition, (2 volumes).
David M. Knipe, Peter M. Howley MD, Diane E. Griffin MD PhD, Robert A. Lamb PhD, Malcolm A. Martin MD, Bernard Roizman, and Stephen E. Straus, editors. 2001. Lippincott Williams & Wilkins Publishers, Baltimore, MD.

Field's Virology is considered the definitive reference about diseases. Without a doubt it's highly technical, presenting in-depth details. A background in medical biology, cell-biology, chemistry, basic genetics, and basic virology is an advantage. Again, as with many other medical and science reference sources, science fiction writers will find these two volumes useful for numerous reasons: perspective on parasitic interactions and invasive organisms, help in understanding the immune systems and how they could be engineered to adapt to different organisms and environments, and even as a method to help generate ideas for alien organisms.

The two-volumes present histories of diseases, contain detailed discussions about infectious agents, pathogenesis and pathology, clinical features, epidemiology, immunity, and methods for controling diseases. The volumes are divided into two sections: the first describes concepts of basic and medical virology; the second details replication, molecular biology, pathogenesis and all medical aspects of individual virus groups.

Forensic Pathology.
Bernard Knight, M.D. 1996. Oxford University Press, USA. New York, NY.

Bernard Knight presents outstanding descriptive commentaries and excellent although very graphic photos in this reference about forensic pathology that's easy-to-read. Note: it's very detailed and, as one reviewer pointed out, it's definitely not one you'll want the kids leafing through. While no significant science background is required, a reasonable familiarity with physiology and anatomy wouldn't hurt.

Here's a quick "FYI": this title is not out of print even though, for some reason, it's listed as such on numerous online bookstores. Consequently, it must be ordered directly from the publisher. Large bookstores probably can look it up and order it for you as well. And, despite my efforts at avoiding internet dependence in my book, *When Digital Isn't Real*, you could actually check out the ordering procedures online by visiting Oxford University Press's website. The downside: it can take anywhere from three to five months to receive your copy.

A few of the fun contents you'll find are chapters about abrasions, punctures and stabbings, drowning, electrical trauma, and child abuse. This reference doesn't duplicate or supplement information in "Medico-legal" research. Rather, its main focus is pathology instead of focusing on details that can be used as support for disproving homicides in defense cases.

Recent Vertebrate Carcasses and Their Paleo-biological Implications.

Johannes Weigelt, Translated by Judith Schaefer. 1989, University of Chicago Press.

This early work prevails as both excellent and useful. Weigelt's book includes drawings and photographs but some basic knowledge of biology and paleontology is recommended. Any writer who plan to include descriptions about decay or remains—especially the murder-mystery writer, is sure to find this book indespensible. Originally, it was published in German in 1927. This reference contains fascinating details and descriptions of decomposition in modern animal carcasses. No dinosaurs here other than the book!

Weigelt describes a range of specific signs that indicate, very reliably, the length of time a carcass has remained undisturbed plus he discusses desiccation and mummification, effects of water, wind, quicksand, mud, and more that defy the imagination.

One surprising tidbit is his description of scavenger activities as well as information about sorting bones based upon weight as carcass remains are eaten. Skip this one before dinner.

Fantastic Trees.
Menninger, Edwin A. 1995 Timber Press, Inc.

This useful, highly accessible reference provides concise high-level information about strange trees from around the world. Even the prologue is interesting. Included are a number of black-and-white photos. Posessing some background in botanical terminology could help but isn't crucial since *Fantastic Trees* was written for the lay-person.

It's often referred to as an "idea" book for science fiction and adventure writers owing to the odd foliage described. There are trees with unusual forms producing strange fruits and weird flowers, bark, roots, leaves, and even offensive odors. Some good examples: I found references to trees with parasitic roots, breathing roots, organ-pipe trees, and several that sported ridiculous names such as bottle trees, cucumber trees, flask trees, pillow stuffers, belly palms, and dragon's blood.

Good fun for the curious even if you end up never using any of the information. No gore here so kids might enjoy this one. My one issue with this source: more photos, especially in color, definitely would have boosted this reference source up a few notches on my list.

A Bit of Chemistry

Book of Poisons: A Guide for Writers.
Stevens, Serita and Anne Bannon. 2007. Writer's Digest Books, Indiana University, IN.

Any writer seeking factual and accurate information about poisonings ought to consult this guide. And fortunately, while not too common, some memoir writers and keepers of the family's secrets may want to review this guide. Not all stories that involve poisonings are fiction "who-dunits." Plenty of real life tales abound—well kept, dark family secrets about suicides and murders, the type committed in gore-free, clean, silent ways. Those depend upon poison, of course!

Book of Poisons is a thorough guide cataloging classic poisons, household poisons, poisonous plants, animals, poisons used in wars and commercial poisons. It even details toxicity levels and reaction times, effects and symptoms, plus available antidotes or treatments. The glossary of medical terms is most helpful to writers without medical backgrounds.

Deadly Doses: A Writer's Guide to Poisons (Howdunit Writing), (First edition).

Serita, Deborah Stevens and Anne Klarner. 1990. Writer's Digest Books.

This superb reference book is perfect for writers who need any information what-so-ever that deals with poison. It contains a short history of poisons plus descriptions in a style representative of the classic mystery writers.

Poisons: From Hemlock to Botox and the Killer Bean of Calabar.

Macginnis, Peter. 2004. Arcade Publishing, Inc., Time-Warner Book Group, New York, NY.

Sometimes the best research we can do involves going somewhere we wouldn't normally go and talking to people we wouldn't normally talk to—and of course, really listening.

-Excerpt From: Brenda Miller & Suzanne Paola.
Tell It Slant, 2nd Edition.

Facts in books, statistics in encyclopedias, the ability to use them in men's heads.

-Fogg Brackell

IIX

Helpful Readings

Specific to Research Methods

The sources listed below are helpful to any writer, regardless of topic, or whether their genre is fiction or non-fiction. I've used these consistently over the years and continue to refer to them often. Several aren't reference books at all, but all the same, they're well worth reading if only on a philosophical level. Besides, they offer an opportunity to alter your perspective about the research process and the true value of accuracy.

<u>Where to Find What: A Handbook to Reference Service</u>,
(4th edition).
Hillard, James M. with Bethany J. Easter. 2000. Scarecrow Press, Inc., Lanham, MA.

<u>The Craft of Research</u>, (2nd edition).
Booth, Wayne C., Gregory G. Colomb, and Joseph M. Williams. 2003. University of Chicago Press, Chicago, IL.

The Lifespan of a Fact.
D'Agata, John and Jim Fingal. 2012. W. W. Norton & Company, New York, NY.

D'Agata is an essayist and writer of creative non-fiction, but has been challenged about exactly how much of his creative non-fiction really is non-fiction. In this book, he and his fact-checker Jim Fingal engage in an intense debate about the meaning of truth and the definition of nonfiction.

Is a "fact," when used in nonfiction writing, ever flexible? In 2003, John D'Agata's essay was rejected by the magazine that had commissioned it. They claimed there were gross inaccuracies.

Eventually, the essay became the basis for his acclaimed article that *The Believer*, a totally different kind of publication accepted and ran. *The Believer* submitted D'Agata's piece to their fact-checker, Jim Fingal. That led to almost seven years filled with arguments and revisions while the two men tried to agree upon what constitutes literary nonfiction.

The Lifespan of a Fact presents D'Agata's original essay plus numerous correspondences between the two authors. The resulting book is a helpful analysis and discussion dealing with the relationship between "truth" and "accuracy." The authors also consider a broader philosophical issue: whether it's ever appropriate for writers to substitute one for the other.

After the Fact: The Art of Historical Detection.
Davidson, James West and Mark Hamilton Lytle. 2003.
McGraw Hill – Higher Education, Madison, WI.

I love this book! The authors raise intriguing questions so often overlooked.

In Fact: The Best of Creative Non-fiction.
Lee Gutkind, Editor 2005. Creative Nonfiction Foundation,
W.W. Norton and Company, Inc. New York, NY.

Really an anthology, but these shorts present excellent examples of creative non-fiction while providing insights into the importance of details.

The Oxford Guide to Library Research.
Mann, Thomas. 2005. Oxford University Press, USA;
New York, NY. *

I summarized the *The Oxford Guide* in section one of this book but list it here for some further discussion. It's definitly helpful reading either way. The site listed here offers electronic access to the guide but it's also available for purchase at online booksellers. Unless you're a wel seasoned researcher, this is one book worth owning. The publisher's quote is one-hundred percent right as far as I'm concerned;

"Essential reading for students, scholars, professional researchers, and laypersons, *The Oxford Guide to Library Research* offers a rich, inclusive overview of the information field, one that can save researchers countless hours of frustration in the search for the best sources on their topics."

One afterthought: learning about the author's background makes this reference guide a bit more fun to use. When I refer to it, I imagine a Sherlock Holmes character. Dr. Mann is a former private investigator who now works as a Reference Librarian in the Main Reading Room of the Library of Congress in Washington, D.C. Not the typical career path of an investigator but research for writing is, after all, very much an investigative activity.

*Download electronic edition at:
www.catdir.loc.gov/catdir/toc

Oral History for the Qualitative Researcher: Choreographing the Story.

Janesick, Valerie J., 2010. The Guilford Press, New York, NY.

The Fourth Genre: Contemporary Writers of and on Creative Nonfiction.

Root, Robert L., and Michael Steinberg. 2002. Longman-Pearson Education, Inc. New York, NY.

Contemporary Creative Nonfiction: The Art of Truth.
Roorbach, Bill. 2001. Oxford University Press,
New York, NY.

Memoir: A History,
Yagoda, Ben. 2009. Riverhead Books, New York, NY.

**The Professional Stranger: An Informal Introduction
to Ethnography**.
Agar, Michael H.1996. Academic Press, New York, NY.

**The Genealogists' Handbook: Modern Methods for
Researching Family History**.
Wright, Raymond S. 1995.

After all, the ultimate goal
of all research is not
objectivity, but truth.

-Helene Deutsch

IX

Specific to Writing a Family History

Breathe Life into Your Life Story: How to Write a Story People Will Want to Read.
Thurston, Dawn and Morris Thurston. 2007. Signature Books, Salt Lake City, UT.

"Showing, not telling," means creating interesting characters and settings, alternating scene and narrative, generating suspense, writing at the gut level, and more (Author's Description).

For All Time: A Complete Guide to Writing Your Family History.
Kempthorne, Charley. 1996. Heinemann, Portsmouth, NH.

Mr. Kempthorne's encouraging style is wise. He makes writing books, if only for family, seem very possible.

Keeping Family Stories Alive: Discovering and Recording the Stories and Reflections of a Lifetime, (Revised edition).
Rosenbluth. Vera. 1997. Hartley and Marks Publishing, Vancouver, British Columbia, Canada.

Interviewing and recording techniques for family histories.

Legacy: A Step-By-Step Guide to Writing Personal History, (First edition).
Spence, Linda. 1997. Swallow Press, Athens, OH.

A popular guide for conducting interviews and writing up oral, personal, and family histories. Ms. Spence includes numerous helpful memory prompts aims at inspiring participants to tell their stories. Even better, the prompts are constructed to help them remember their stories.

Living Legacies: How to Write, Illustrate, and Share Your Life Stories.
Elgin, Duane and Colleen Ledrew. 2001. Conari Press, Newburyport, MA.

This guide will be helpful to anyone writing memoirs or their own life's stories, but it's especially helpful if you're working on a family history. *Living Legacies* contains valuable tips about how to illustrate stories with photographs, memorabilia, and other images. I was drawn to suggestions about how those same images can serve as writing prompts, a particularly helpful guide for writers new to memoir.

Story Bridges: A Guide for Conducting Intergenerational Oral History Projects.
Zusman. Angela. 2010. Left Coast Press, Walnut Creek, CA.

Oral history projects are excellent educational opor tunities. The concept and process described are ones all schools and families might want to consider.

The Dead Beat: Lost Souls, Lucky Stiffs, and the Perverse Pleasures of Obituaries.
Johnson. Marilyn. 2007. Harper Perennial Books, New York, NY.

Dead Beat is a fun, unconventional approach to explaining how our final stories finally get told.

To Our Children's Children: Preserving Family Histories for Generations to Come.
Greene, Bob. 1993. Doubleday, New York, NY.

A small book filled with writing prompts for oral or written family histories—one of the earlier books of its kind.

You Can Write Your Family History.
Carmack, Sharon DeBartolo, 2009. Genealogical
Publishing, Baltimore, MD.

Starting from a genealogy base, Carmack offers tips about bringing characters and social history to life and presenting stories about people on the family tree.

Prove all things, hold fast to that which is true.

– The Bible. 1 Thessalonians 5:21

X

Specific to Writing a Personal Memoir

The Legacy Guide: Capturing the Facts, Memories, and Meaning of Your Life.
Franco, Carol and Kent Lineback. 2006. Tarcher Publishing, New York, NY.

Moving from facts to memories to meaning, the authors take you through seven life stages – childhood, adolescence, young adulthood (roughly 20-30), adulthood (roughly 30-45), middle adulthood (roughly 45-60), late adulthood (roughly 60-80), elder (roughly 80 onward) – inviting you to recall forgotten moments and discover their significance (Publishers' Description).

The Memoir Project: A Thoroughly Non-Standardized Text for Writing and Life.
Smith, Marion Roach. 2011. Grand Central Publishing; New York, NY.

Everyone has stories to tell, but writer and memoir writing instructor Marion Roach Smith says making our stories both interesting and readable is harder than it might seem. Her new book is totally honest and filled with quirky, provocative tactics. All are aimed at teaching you how to write with purpose.

Turning Memories into Memoirs: A Handbook for Writing Life-Stories.
Ledoux, Denis. 2005. Soleil Press, Lisbon Falls, ME.

Denis Ledoux's book is regarded as a "workshop in a book," offering encouragment to non-writers about how to write their own stories. Of course, there's no reason writers can't also benefit form those suggestions.

Writing Life Stories: How to Make Memories into Memoirs, Ideas into Essays, and Life into Literature.
Roorbach, Bill. 1998. Story Press, Cincinnati, OH.

The Heart and Craft of Lifestory Writing: How to Transform Memories Into Meaningful Stories.
Lippincott. Sharon. 2007. Lighthouse Point Press, Pittsburgh, PA.

Lippincott presents no-nonsense practical advice for writing and publishing life stories.

Old Friend from Far Away: The Practice of Writing Memoir.
Goldberg, Natalie. 2009. Atria Books - Simon & Schuster, New York, NY.

"To write memoir," Goldberg says, "we must first know how to remember." Through timed, associative, and meditative exercises, *Old Friend from Far Away* guides you to the attentive state of thought—a place in which you will discover and open those forgotten doors of memory.

Thinking About Memoir.
Thomas, Abigail. 2008. Sterling Publishing, New York, NY.

A small volume of writing prompts, *Thinking about Memoir* encourages writers to write "briefs". Thomas is a fan of coming at your life through the side door, an approach she used in her own memoir, *Safekeeping: Some True Stories from a Life.* She shows us that vignettes, artfully arranged, can convey the arc of changing relationships.

You Are Next In Line: Everyone's Guide for Writing Your Autobiography.
Jagoe, Armiger. 2007. Capital Books, Dulles, VA.

This simple, do-it-yourself guide contains excerpts from famous life stories as an approach to illustrating specific life themes, for instance: In the Beginning, Family Affairs, First Home, Grown Up, Adult Life, Special People, Important Events and Life Passages. I think Jagoe's guide is appropriate for memoir writing beginers.

Your Life As Story: Discovering the New Autobiography.
Rainer, Tristine. 1998. Tarcher-Putnam Books, New York, NY.

Rainer's guide is well organized—not much fluff in this one. She included numerous well thought out examples from her own life story plus solutions to problems her students typically encounter in their own writing.

Facts in all their glorious complexity make possible creativity.

- Philip Gerard

XI

Specific to Writing Healing Memoirs

Another Morning: Voices of Truth and Hope from Mothers with Cancer.
Blachman, Linda. 2006. Seal Press, Berkeley, CA.

Another Morning was written and organized in an effort to inspire seriously ill parents to write and leave stories and messages for their survivors.

Coyote Wisdom: The Power of Story in Healing.
Mehl-Madrona, Lewis. 2005. Bear and Company, Rochester, VT.

This book provides an in-depth look at the therapeutic and transformative powers of storytelling in Native American and several other cultures. The author explores the process of creating a "healing state of mind" through the use of stories.

Fearless Confessions: A Writer's Guide to Memoir.
Silverman, Sue Williams. 2009. University of Georgia Press,
Athens, GA.

Silverman has a mission: encourage writers to transform their life stories, no matter how traumatic, into words that do matter. By writing, she contends, they can find the courage to speak truth about issues others might prefer to keep secret.

Living to Tell the Tale: A Guide to Writing Memoir.
Jane Taylor McDonnell. 1998. Penguin Books,
New York, NY.

How to write "crisis memoirs," is all about – as the author contends, finding "...our own meaningfulness, even in the midst of sadness and disappointment."

Narrative Medicine.
Rita Charon. 2008. Oxford University Press, New York, NY.

A doctor's job is to listen to patients' stories and to know more about the patient than medical charts can convey. Encouraging patients to write often helps with the healing process and can offer care providers insight into their patients' illnesses.

Narrative Medicine is considered a practical guide for implementing narrative methods in health care.

The author, who was trained both in medicine and literary studies, comes to her expertise with wonderful insights.

Opening Up: The Healing Power of Expressing Emotions.
Pennebaker, James W. 1997. The Guilford Press, New York, NY.

In controlled clinical research funded by the National Science Foundation and the National Institutes of Health, Pennebaker presents advanced data about the powerful mind/body connection. This book chronicles evidence that personal self-disclosure is beneficial both emotional health and boosts physical health.

The Healing Art of Storytelling,
Stone, Richard. 2005. Authors Choice Press, Lincoln, NE.

The Illness Narratives.
Kleinman, Arthur. 1989. Basic Books, New York, NY.

Based upon twenty years of clinical experience studying and treating chronic illness Kleinman, a Harvard psychiatrist and anthropologist, argues that diagnosing illness is an art often neglected in modern medical training. He presents a compelling case for bridging the gap between patients and doctors through the method of narratives and story.

The Power of Memoir: How to Write Your Healing Story.
Myers, Linda Joy. 2010. Jossey-Bass Publishers, San Francisco, CA.

All about step-by-step memoir writing, with the goal of healing from emotional pain.

The Story of Your Life: Becoming the Author of Your Experience.
Aftel, Mandy. 1997. Touchstone, New York, NY.

Ms. Aftel asks the reader to reflect upon three major life plots (love, mastery, and loss). These exercises ask us to reflect about events such as: How Money Complicates the Love Plot, How Children Complicate the Marriage Plot, and How Escape Complicates the Mastery Plot. The author contends that trite or destructive story lines might be crafted into original narratives focused on courage, fulfillment, and imagination.

The Wounded Storyteller: Body, Illness, and Ethics.
Arthur Frank. 2013. University of Chicago Press, Chicago, IL.

Frank recounts a stirring collection of illness stories that range from the well-known—Gilda Radner's battle with ovarian cancer, to private testimonials from people with cancer, chronic fatigue syndrome, and disabilities.

The stories are more than simple accounts of personal suffering. They detail the nature and impotrance of moral choices and point to a "social ethic."

Vertigo: A Memoir (The Cross-Cultural Memoir Series).
DeSalvo, Louise. 2002. The Feminist Press at CUNY, New York, NY.

Controversial scholar-critic Louise DeSalvo breaks the traditional silence around life for an Italian American girl coming of age. She sifts through painful memories of childhood incest, a sister's suicide, and other traumas.

If your sources are wrong, you are wrong. You are responsible for the information in your story, however you attribute it. Do all you can to evaluate the source and verify the information.

-Judith Miller, *New York Times.*

XII

Books That Exemplify Excellent Research

<u>The Lost: A Search for Six of Six Million</u>,
Mendelsohn, Daniel. 2007. Harper Perennial,
New York, NY.

Daniel Mendelsohn chronicles his travels to the now decimated Eastern European villages that once were the centers of Jewish learning and culture. His travels are part of the research he immerses himself in as he tries to find information about members of his family.

In addition to traveling to lost villages and interviewing elderly local residents, his research also takes him to Sidney, Australia and Jerusalem, Israel. But one of the unusual uses of his research is that the author makes the research process an important part of the story itself.

<u>**My Father's Paradise: A Son's Search for His Jewish Past**</u>
<u>**in Kurdish Iraq**</u>.
> Saber, Arie. 2009. Algonquin Books, Chapel Hill, NC.

<u>**Blood Work: A Tale of Medicine and Murder in the Scientific**</u>
<u>**Revolution**</u>.
> Tucker, Holly. 2012. W. W. Norton & Company,
> New York, NY.

Genealogy Research Sites

Even though my purpose in writing this book was to focus upon printed and publicly available "real world" reference materials, I simply couldn't manage without including at least a few very specific and highly reliable websites.

Sure, there are plenty of books and materials that can offer help to writers involved with genealogy research, but primarily they instruct would-be genealogists in research methods. They help design strategies, and sequential proceedures.

The sites that follow offer a good deal of helpful advice about process and contain very precise information that can be accessed in files, records, and historical data at the individual level. Note, while many more are available, those listed are reputable and have been up and running for many years.

www.familysearch.org

www.archives.gov/genealogy/

www.ancestry.com/home

www.rootsweb.com

www.usgenweb.org/research/index.shtml

www.jewishgen.org/databases/

www.ellisisland.org

Know where to find the information and how to use it - that's the secret of success.

Albert Einstein, German-born American Physicist;
Nobel Prize for Physics in 1921.

Accuracy is the foundation upon which writers must build all other skills.

-Steve Buttry, *The Buttry Diary.*

XIII

Some Extra Helpful Places and Resources

Archives Departments

Most colleges and universities collect and maintain photographs, articles and publications pertaining to their graduates and faculty members, as well as their regional history. In addition, many schools have more specialized holdings, for example: University of Chicago Libraries contain extensive materials focused on development of the Midwest. Also, they specialize in historical maps and atlases plus very extensive histories about the great Columbia Exposition. Another example of a highly specialized collection can be found in the archives department of Holy Cross College in Massachusetts. It maintains very detailed information about the Irish population of Worcester.

One extra bit of information—almost all libraries participate in a program referred to as "inter-library loan." Consequently, if you're aware of a reference that isn't available at your local library, often times it can be obtained for you by the librarian through the inter-library loan program. Included at the end of my book is a copy of a typical inter-library loan request form in the public domain.

Newspapers

All large, and some small, city newspapers maintain archives dating back ten years or more. These are accessible online and through most public libraries. It's possible to order older articles although some may require small fees. Historical pieces generally are available on microfilm or in print. Many newspapers maintain "on-site" files and accept requests from researchers for individual assistance usually on an appointment basis.

Periodical Indexes

Readers' Guide to Periodicals includes references to all popular magazines such as *Newsweek, Time Magazine, Good Housekeeping* and most mass market publications.

The Readers' Guide to Periodical Literature is a reference guide to recently published articles that appear in both periodical magazines and in scholarly journals. It's organized on the basis of article subjects. Published since 1901 by The H. W. Wilson Company, the guide has been—and continues to be, an important staple of almost every American library. Retrospective indexes to this same category of periodicals published between 1890 to 1982 also are available.

Two online database versions of *Reader's Guide* are available at The H. W. Wilson Company's website. These provide valuable supplemental information; *The Readers' Guide to Periodical Literature Retrospective (1890-1982)* and an updated version that focuses on 1983 to the present.

This guide book is the best resource for finding primary source documents published between 1900 and 1984. Besides, it's probably the only index in which to find articles that were published by popular magazines during most of the 20th century.

In this book, I've pointed out that not all research can be accomplished online. The major reason *Reader's Guide* is such a valuable reference—one confirmed by The H. W. Wilson Company, is that there's a huge time gap in what's available and accessible online and what can be found in print. One problem I'm sure you'll encounter, and a good example of the time gap is finding any information from periodicals online that pertains to the 1920's through the 1970's.

Specialized References

Numerous indexes that focus on very narrow fields are published annually. Some examples are: *The Music Index, Who's Who In Science, Index of Patents*, and *Popular American Songs*, but literally there are probably thousands of these.While some are available online, most are in print at larger public libraries and universities.

A world of facts lies
outside and beyond
the world of words.

-Thomas Henry Huxley

XIV

The "Oft' Overlooked" - Unconventional Sources

Those of us who do spend huge blocks of time conducting research usually tend—first and foremost, to begin our work with an internet search. It's only after that when we begin to think about referring to books, or searching libraries. We may even seek out some expert advice. That's all fine but writers and researchers tend to overlook, almost entirely, sources they don't consider to be reference materials.

You will see from my following list, data can be obtained from a wide range of unconventional, yet common, sources. I've categorized these into two distinct groups. These are based upon my own experiences of having tried to find detailed historical information. First, there are references most often regarded as public sources. Then the second category of resources–and one generally bypassed, is the vast range of private documents and collections.

I've listed a number of examples of information sources I use but there surely must be more that never occurred to me. Let your imagination be your inspiration. If you're facing a roadblock, this could be a good time to ask yourself, "Just what would Sherlock Holmes do? Where would he look?"

Public Sources

This category of information really is accessible to anyone and most likely is readily available in libraries, museums, publications, and governmental offices. It includes newspapers, magazines, books, journals, internet sources, tax records, census data, economic indexes, art and artifacts, and just about anything not protected by privacy laws.

Private Sources

Exactly as my heading above states, these resources are private—either because they're privately owned or the information is protected by privacy laws. Information and materials are owned by families, individuals, and sometimes organizations and corporations. Permission to obtain access always is required. Items of interest to researchers might include personal correspondences, diaries, photographs, journals, scrapbooks, memorabilia, personal interviews, and even audio recordings, slides and film clips.

Overlooked Sources

Adoption records

Antiques

Automobiles

Bills of sale

Birth certificates

Blueprints

Books

Catalogues

City guide books

Clothing articles

Collectables

Commercials or advertising

Commercial products

Cookbooks or recipe collections

Educational curricula

Entertaining invitations

Financial records

Health records

Household items

Interviews

Jewelry

Labor statistics

Legal documents

Magazines

Maps

Menus

Movies, television shows
and theatre performances

Museums

Music - written or recorded

Paintings and art

Photographs

Political campaign slogans
and mementos

Regional census files

Religious sermons and practices

School yearbooks

Ship and airplane manifests

Superstitions, taboos and fads

Transportation records

Travel brochures

Voting and tax records

A Final Note In Closing

If you, dear reader, come up with more ideas,
I hope you'll email me at marlenesamuels@gmail.com

Thank You!

SAMPLE INTERLIBRARY LOAN REQUEST

Before submitting this request, please be sure to check our online catalog for this journal's online availability.

PLEASE PRINT CLEARLY!
Today's Date:_____

Your Name:_____
Email:_____

I would like my article delivered via: Paper_____ Email:_____
(UNH email preferred)

Title of Article: _____

Author(s) of Article: _____

Journal Title (No Abbreviations): _____

Volume:_____ Issue Number:_____ Date:_____
Pages:_____

Professor's Name & Course:_____
_____

Some libraries charge a fee for copying. Are you willing to pay for this article*?
YES   NO
*Please Note: If there is a charge, we will always notify you.

NOTICE: WARNING CONCERNING COPYRIGHT RESTRICTIONS
        Photocopies and other reproductions can be furnished under certain conditions, if they will be used solely for private scholarship or research. Use of the reproduction for any other purposes may make the user liable for copyright infringement... This institution reserves the right to refuse to accept a copying order if, in its judgment, fulfillment of the order would involve violation of the copyright law.
Verified:_____ ISSN:_____

About Marlene Samuels

Marlene Samuels is a writer, independent research sociologist, and an instructor. She earned both her M.A. and Ph.D. degrees from University of Chicago where currently she serves on the Visiting Committee to the Social Sciences. She has been a longtime member of the University of Chicago's Women's Board.

When not writing short stories or creating recipes for her culinary blog, *www.anotherdaygourmet.com*, Marlene conducts research methodology workshops. Research is a skill she believes is overlooked much too often but one that's critical for writers to master if they hope to establish credibility in their writing. She also teaches workshops that focus on memoir writing methods. Marlene is a guest lecturer and also moderates at independent book clubs.

Marlene is a member of Story Circle Network. She serves on their board of directors and is Program Director. She's a member of AROHO Foundation (A Room of Her Own Foundation) and a participant, presenter, and consultant at their Ghost Ranch Writers' Retreat in Abiquiu, New Mexico.

Her work appears in publications like *Lilith Magazine, The Chicago Tribune, ReadyMade Magazine, University of Iowa Summer Writing Anthology, Story Circle Anthology, A Long Story Short, L.A. Review*, and a variety of e-zines and journals. Marlene co-authored and edited her mother's WW-II memoir, *The Seamstress: A Memoir of Survival*, Penguin-Berkley Press and is completing her book, *Broken Chains, Missing Links: A Memoir Told In Short Stories*.

Marlene is available to conduct workshops and make presentations.

Learn about Marlene's areas of expertise, scheduling, and read excerpts of her writing at:

marlenesamuels.com

marlenesamuels.blogspot.com

Facebook

www.facebook.com/marlene.samuels

About Jeff Potter

Jeff Potter is a freelance visual designer and illustrator currently residing in Pasadena, CA. Jeff has designed numerous sites and materials for Marlene's other projects including

www.marlenesamuels.com

www.anotherdaygourmet.com

He is available for interesting projects.

View his work at:

www.jbrianpotter.com

jbrianpotter@gmail.com

Twitter: @jbrianpotter

All reviews written, edited, and curated by
Marlene Samuels.

Cover design and interior layout by Jeff Potter.

Body copy set in Times Regular
Headings set in Trade Gothic